SERIES 218

In this book, we explore what electricity is, how it is created and how it is used, and we meet the scientists who helped to bring electrical power to the people.

LADYBIRD BOOKS

UK | USA | Canada | Ireland | Australia
India | New Zealand | South Africa

Ladybird Books is part of the Penguin Random House group of companies whose addresses can be found at global.penguinrandomhouse.com.

www.penguin.co.uk   www.puffin.co.uk   www.ladybird.co.uk

Penguin
Random House
UK

First published 2021
001

Printed in China

The authorized representative in the EEA is Penguin Random House Ireland, Morrison Chambers, 32 Nassau Street, Dublin D02 YH68

A CIP catalogue record for this book is available from the British Library

ISBN: 978-0-241-41694-5

All correspondence to:
Ladybird Books
Penguin Random House Children's
One Embassy Gardens, 8 Viaduct Gardens
London SW11 7BW

Electricity

A Ladybird Book

Written by Elizabeth Jenner
with physics consultant, Heloise Chomet

Illustrated by Brave the Woods

What is electricity?

Almost everything we do each day relies on something called "electricity" – from cooking meals and lighting buildings to keeping in touch with friends and watching films and television programmes. But what is electricity?

To understand electricity, we must first look at one of the smallest building blocks of life: the atom. Atoms are invisible to the human eye, but anything that can be touched is made from these miniscule objects – from elephants and humans to mountains and rivers. They are everywhere!

Atoms are made up of protons, neutrons and electrons. Protons and neutrons clump together in the middle of an atom to form a nucleus. The electrons float around, or "orbit", the nucleus, held in place by their charge.

A charge is a quality, much like weight or size. Charges can be positive, negative or neutral. In the case of atoms, the protons are positively charged, the electrons are negatively charged and the neutrons are neutral.

Opposite charges attract, which means the electrons are attracted to the protons. However, electrons can jump from atom to atom if they find a stronger positive charge elsewhere. It is the movement of electrons that creates an electric current and, therefore, power and electricity.

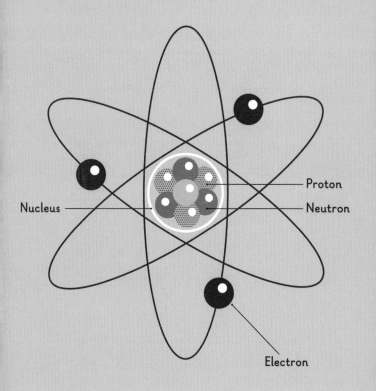

Proton

Nucleus

Neutron

Electron

Conductors and insulators

Conductors are materials that allow electricity to flow through them easily. The atoms in conductors have a weak structure, which makes it easy for electrons to move and for a current to flow through the material.

A lot of metals, such as iron and copper, are conductors. Fine strands of copper and iron are often used to make the wires for carrying electricity and to power electrical devices. Other more unusual conductors include seawater, lemon juice and the plasma cells in blood!

While conductors help the flow of electricity, insulators are materials that do not allow electricity to pass through them. The atoms of insulators have a strong structure, making it very difficult, or even impossible, for the electrons to move – a bit like the way it is difficult to cycle when a bicycle has its brakes on. As the electrons cannot move, the electric charge cannot flow.

Plastic is a good insulator, which is why it is often wrapped around wires that carry electricity. The plastic keeps the electric charge inside the wire and protects people from the charge. Other insulating materials include rubber, glass and oil.

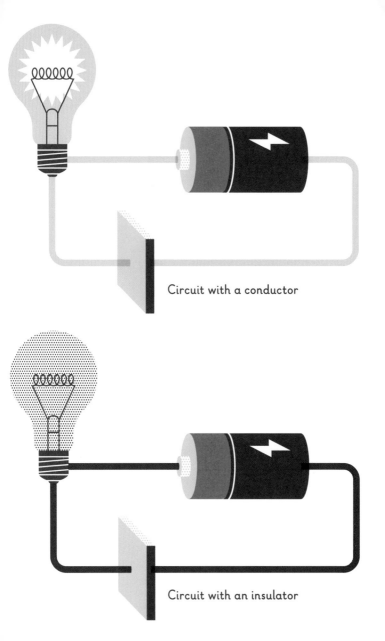

Circuit with a conductor

Circuit with an insulator

Static electricity

Static electricity is the build-up of electrical energy. Unlike current, which flows, static electricity gathers in one place.

The first people to discover static electricity were the ancient Greeks. They realized that they could create static electricity by rubbing different materials together. A modern example of this can be found at a birthday party. If you rub a balloon on your jumper and then hold the balloon to your chest, it should stick. This is not magic – it's static electricity!

The atoms in the rubber balloon attract electrons more strongly than those in the wool of the jumper. So, as you rub the two materials together, the electrons from the wool jump over to the rubber in the balloon. As a result, the jumper becomes positively charged, and the balloon becomes negatively charged. Because opposites attract, the two materials then stick together!

Another example of static electricity in action is the slight shock you might feel when touching a metal door handle. This is static electricity discharging. You may have built up a positive or negative charge in your body by walking across nylon or woollen carpet. When you touch the metal door handle, that charge suddenly has somewhere to go, so it jumps to the handle, creating a small spark. It might produce a surprising shock, but this small charge is not dangerous.

Electrical storms

Dark clouds gather over Lake Maracaibo in Venezuela. There is a flash and a rumble as a jagged white light zigzags towards the ground. This is an electrical storm, otherwise known as "thunder and lightning". Lake Maracaibo is one of the best places to study thunder and lightning, as it experiences roughly 260 electrical storms every year.

Many myths and legends surround the origins of storms. In Norse folklore, the wheels of the god Thor's chariot cause the rumble of thunder, and the lightning comes from his mighty hammer. In South Africa, some tribes believe that lightning marks the arrival of the *impundulu* (lightning bird), which comes to earth to lay its magical eggs.

Lightning is caused by static electricity in the clouds. Rising water droplets and small ice particles inside the storm clouds rub against soft hail, building up a charge. The water and ice particles become positively charged, and the heavier hail becomes negatively charged.

The static electricity is then released between clouds, or to different parts of the same cloud, causing flashes in the sky. It can also be attracted to the ground, or an object near the ground, causing the charge to zip down and strike the earth with a streak of light.

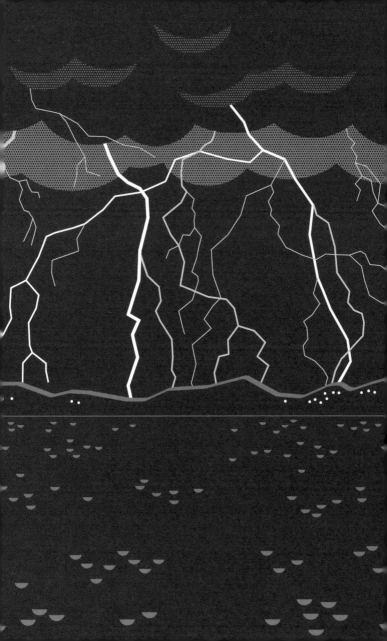

Animal power

Long before people knew how to create and use electricity, they were aware of its existence in nature. Electrical storms were bright, crashing displays of natural electricity, but the ancient Egyptians found a splashier source. They knew that if they were to touch the fish known as the "Thunderer of the Nile", they would get a sharp shock!

This creature is now more commonly known as the "electric catfish". Fish like the electric catfish and the electric eel are able to generate an electric field around their bodies, in a process called "bioelectrogenesis". They use electricity to protect themselves against predators, stun and kill prey, communicate with other fish and find their way around.

These fish have special cells in their bodies that work like batteries – creating, storing and releasing electricity into the body. When the fish's nervous system releases certain chemicals, it activates the electricity. Eighty per cent of an electric eel's body is used to make electricity, and it can produce a shock powerful enough to knock a horse down!

Many other fish, such as sharks and lampreys, also have this superpower. They use their electric fields to sense objects around them, which comes in useful as they hunt in dark, deep water.

Benjamin Franklin's kite

One afternoon in 1752, storm clouds gathered over the city of Philadelphia in the United States of America. As most people ran inside to escape the rain, a scientist called Benjamin Franklin prepared to fly a kite.

Franklin was hoping to conclusively prove that electricity could be found within lightning. He had been waiting for the perfect weather conditions to carry out his experiment. Franklin placed a metal wire at the top of a kite to attract the electrical charge in the storm. Then, he attached a string made of hemp to the kite and tied a metal key to the other end, holding on to his contraption using a silk string.

This unusual kite was then launched during the storm, and it attracted a charge from the lightning. The charge travelled down the wet hemp string to the key, which then became charged with electricity. Franklin was the first person to create a "lightning conductor".

Lightning conductors are now used on tall buildings all around the world. They are specifically designed to attract lightning, as they allow electric charges to pass through buildings safely and enter the ground without harming the structure of the buildings or the people within them.

Powerful people

After Benjamin Franklin's kite experiment proved that electricity could be controlled and used, other scientists started to investigate this new form of energy, too.

Early experiments with electricity proved tricky, as there was no way for scientists to create a safe, predictable charge. So, in 1800, Italian scientist Alessandro Volta created the world's first battery. He soaked paper in salt water and then put zinc and copper on either side. This created a chemical reaction, which produced electricity. Volta's discovery is the reason we measure battery power in "volts".

French scientist André-Marie Ampère discovered that metal wires can attract or repel each other depending on the direction that electricity flows through them. He was one of the first scientists to study electric currents and fields. Through his research, he created Ampère's Law, which describes how current works. In his honour, "ampere" became a unit of electrical measurement.

The English scientist Michael Faraday also experimented with electric power. He discovered that passing a magnet through a copper wire creates an electric current. This method is used today to generate electricity in power plants.

1. Volta's battery
2. Lightning rod
3. Franklin's kite
4. Ammeter
5. Faraday disc

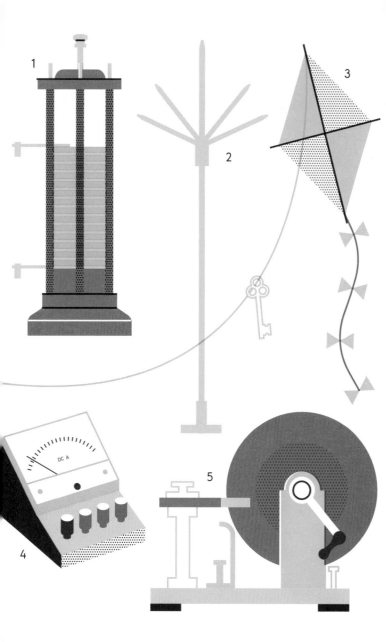

Improving electricity

One of the first uses for electricity was to provide light. However, the first electric lights were expensive, short-lived and impractical. Thomas Edison, an American engineer, developed the first long-lasting light bulb, using a cotton filament – a conducting thread – that did not burn out.

In 1827, Georg Ohm discovered that the amount of current flowing through an electrical object is related to the strength of the power source. For example, if an electric circuit contains a lot of lights, the bulbs will be duller because they share a power source. If you reduce the number of lights, the bulbs will have more power and will shine brighter.

Heinrich Hertz was the first scientist to notice that sparks of electricity were able to jump through gaps in circuits. Using this idea, he used an electric charge to send electronic waves across his laboratory. This research would go on to spark the invention of the radio, and sound-wave frequency is now measured in "hertz" in his honour.

The engineer Nikola Tesla invented a method of supplying electricity using the "Tesla coil". His "alternating current" transformed electric charge into a high-voltage, low-current type of electricity that was then used around the world.

1. AC motor
2. Radio
3. Ohm's law
4. Light bulb
5. Electrochemical cell
6. Tesla coil

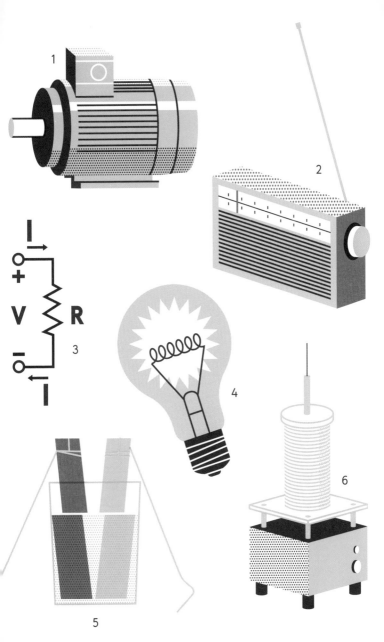

1

2

V R 3

4

5

6

Storing electricity: batteries

We need electrical energy to power anything electronic, including phones, torches, tablets and laptops. But it is not always possible, or practical, to connect these items to a mains power source. Instead, these devices have batteries inside them so they can be used anywhere.

A battery is a container filled with chemicals. These chemicals are able to create electricity over a long period of time and can release the charge slowly, as and when it is needed.

Batteries have three parts: a positive terminal (the "cathode"), a negative terminal (the "anode") and the chemical solution between them, called the "electrolyte".

Chemical reactions in the liquid electrolyte cause a build-up of negative electrons at the anode. The electrons are attracted to the positive cathode, but as they are unable to move through the electrolyte, their electrical energy becomes stored instead.

When the battery is placed within a circuit, the electrons in the anode are able to reach the cathode by going the long way round and flowing through the circuit! Electricity flows through the wires, powering whatever else is connected within the circuit, such as a light bulb.

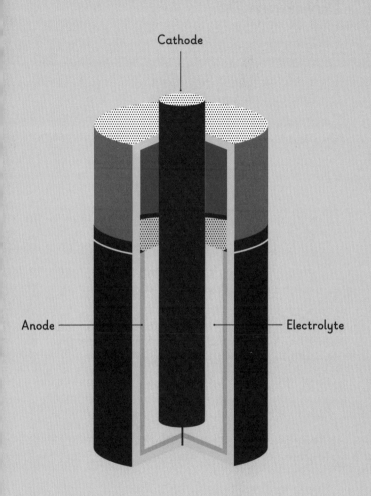

Cathode

Anode

Electrolyte

Direct current

Electricity that flows in one direction around a circuit is called "direct current", or "DC". It moves constantly from a negatively charged place, where there are many electrons, to a positively charged place, where there are fewer of them. If you use a battery-operated device, it probably uses a direct current, with the charge travelling around a smaller circuit.

Thomas Edison introduced the direct current system in 1882, when he built the first power plant in New York City. It was designed to create, or "generate", power and send it directly into people's homes. However, Edison's direct current only worked well when it travelled short distances. This meant that only people who lived near the power plant, roughly 85 customers, could use the electric power.

Edison's circuit was soon evolved and expanded upon, and today, high-voltage direct current (HVDC) allows a direct current to travel much further. Electricity is transferred through overhead lines, and also cables on the seabed, making electricity available to more people around the world. It is a lot cheaper to carry a direct current at a high voltage over long distances, particularly between countries and continents, than it is to build power stations everywhere.

Alternating current

Once Thomas Edison's first power plant was in operation, the demand for electric power grew. More and more people wanted to light their homes with electric lamps. However, as we have learned, electricity supplied by the plant could only travel short distances because it was a direct-current system.

To combat this problem, Nikola Tesla designed a new style of current that would be able to provide more people with electricity. Unlike direct current, where electrons always flow in the same direction, Tesla's alternating current, or "AC", allowed electrons to flow backwards and forwards. This flow could also be increased, decreased and controlled using a device known as a "transformer".

Alternating current was a cheaper way to supply and control electricity over longer distances, and to a larger number of people. As the electric-power industry grew, this competition sparked the "War of Currents" between direct and alternating systems.

Eventually, alternating current proved to be the most popular and the most practical. Alternating current is still the most common electrical system used around the world today, providing electricity to homes, schools and offices.

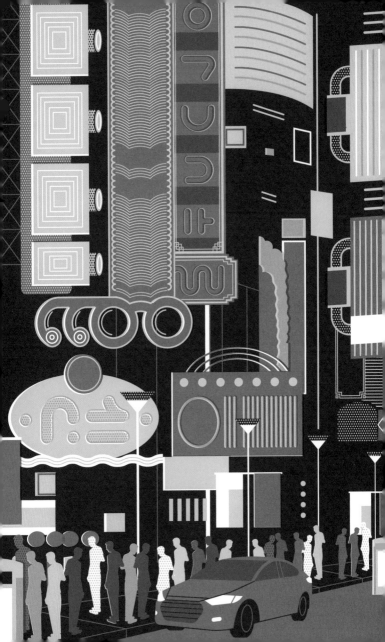

Living with electricity

Once engineers had solved the problem of supply, electricity use boomed. It was used for entertainment, lighting and in a new communication technology – telegraphs. Electric current was used to control a set of magnetized needles that could tap out messages. Communications could then be sent through wires across the country in a matter of hours, which meant that people no longer had to wait for the post. Eventually, the telegraph was replaced by the telephone and, later, the mobile phone.

But even today, there are times when the electricity supply stops. Sometimes electrical equipment is damaged, either by weather, a big electrical surge through the power grid, or by humans – both accidentally and on purpose.

When the electricity supply stops, buildings that rely on an electrical supply, like hospitals, use emergency electricity generators. Generators allow them to keep important machines and services running to help keep people alive.

However, most people must simply wait until the electricity supply comes back on. It's a good idea to keep candles and battery-powered torches in your home – in a place that is easy to find in the dark – in case the electricity stops!

Electricity and fossil fuels

Most of the electricity that we use to power our homes and businesses comes from big power plants, where fuel is converted into power.

1. Most power plants create electricity with "fossil fuels" – natural materials, such as coal or natural gas, mined from beneath the earth's surface. These fuels are transported to power plants, where they are burned to produce heat.

2. The burning fuel heats a boiler of water to produce steam. As the steam rises, it flows around the blades of a turbine and turns them to create mechanical energy.

3. As the blades turn, they drive the attached electrical generator. Inside the generator, copper wire rotates through a strong magnetic field. The wire's movement through the magnetic field causes the electrons to move and create an electric charge. This charge is collected and sent out of the power plant as electricity.

4. Some power plants have huge cooling towers outside them. These help to speed up the electricity production process by cooling the water from the steam turbine. Once the water has cooled inside the tower, it is pumped back into the boiler to be reheated and reused.

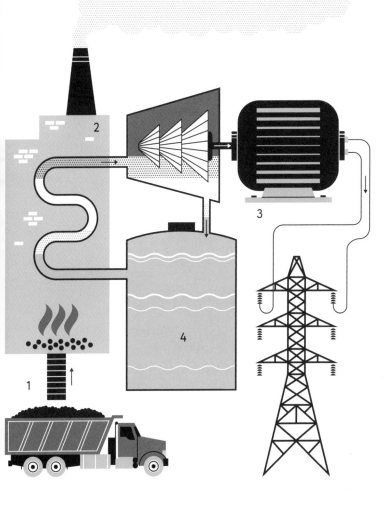

1

2

3

4

Nuclear energy

In the 1930s, scientists discovered that they could use neutrons to split up the centre of an atom, known as the "nucleus". Splitting atoms creates an enormous amount of heat – a vital component in creating electricity. This process is called "nuclear fission". In a controlled environment, using a material with a large nucleus, such as uranium, nuclear fission can be used to produce a huge amount of heat very quickly.

The first power plant to use nuclear energy opened in 1954. Nuclear power plants create electricity in a similar way to fossil fuel plants, but the heat energy is created by nuclear fission instead.

The main benefit of nuclear power is its speed. Not a lot of material is needed in order to generate a large amount of power, so it is a very effective "fuel". In addition, the fission process does not require burning, which means that it doesn't cause air pollution.

However, nuclear reactions create radioactive nuclear waste, which can cause enormous damage to humans and the environment if it isn't stored correctly, or if it is disposed of incorrectly. The risk of devastating accidents occurring is much higher within nuclear power plants. Powerful nuclear explosions can be deadly, and the effects of a nuclear explosion can last for decades.

Renewable energy

Renewable energy comes from something that is unlikely to run out. Fossil fuels, like coal, are non-renewable. This means that once they are burned for energy, they cannot be used again. It is much better for the environment — and for our future — if renewable energy sources are used instead. It helps to prevent climate change.

Wind power can be harnessed to create electricity using tall wind turbines that look a bit like windmills. As the blades of the turbine are blown round by the wind, they power electrical generators. Wind turbines are effective in windy places, but they can be noisy and quite slow.

Solar power is energy generated from the sun. Light particles from the sun, called "photons", are collected by solar panels. These panels contain special cells that allow photons to knock electrons free from atoms. The metal plates at the side of each cell then create a flow of electricity that can be used to power devices.

Hydroelectric power plants use fast-flowing water to turn water turbines that create electricity. Some plants require large amounts of water, which is why a dam might be built on a river to create a temporary reservoir. A dam allows the plant to control how much water is used, and therefore how much electric charge is created.

Power to the people

Today, it is hard to imagine our lives without electricity. In many countries, large electricity networks, or "grids", criss-cross over the land. Electricity is carried through overhead lines and under the ground to homes and businesses everywhere.

When electricity is generated at a power plant, it flows through transformers to increase the voltage. This is an important step, as it makes the electricity more powerful so it can be pushed over longer distances.

This high-voltage electricity travels through power lines until it reaches a substation. Here, the electricity passes through another transformer to now decrease the voltage and make it less powerful. The electricity is then sent on again, through smaller power lines. Before entering homes, the electricity travels through yet another transformer to make the voltage low enough for humans to use safely.

In some places, access to electricity is still limited. In countries where there are fewer power stations, or where people live in remote places, electricity supply is still a luxury. Even if electricity supply exists, it may not be reliable, and people cannot always afford to buy it.

The power inside a plug

In order to watch TV, charge your phone or use a toaster, you need a controlled source of electricity. This comes from the plug sockets that can be found all over your home. Plug sockets provide a connection to an electrical source that is ready to use whenever you need it. When you plug in an appliance, it completes the electric circuit.

Most sockets have three holes that connect to the three separate wires hidden inside the plug. The "live" wire carries the electric current to the plugged-in appliance. The "neutral" wire carries the current away from the appliance again. The "earth" wire directs any dangerous electrical charges safely towards the ground.

The live wire is also connected to a "fuse" inside the plug. This is another safety device, which is able to break the circuit if a dangerously high electric charge passes through the wire. The fuse helps to prevent electrical fires.

Most electricity supplied to homes is on an alternating current system. However, countries all over the world have developed their own electricity systems. This means that the design, voltage and current frequencies in plugs can differ between countries. This is why people often need to attach converters to their plugs when they travel abroad.

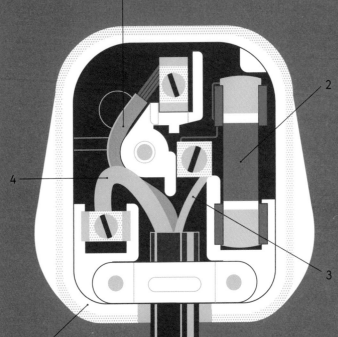

1. Plug casing
2. Fuse
3. Live wire
4. Neutral wire
5. Earth wire

Electrical safety

Electricity is very useful but it can also be very dangerous.
It can start fires, hurt the human body and even kill.
To avoid shocks, never poke anything into the holes
of an electrical socket or make holes in a wall where
a wire might be present.

Water is a good conductor of electricity, and if electrical
devices get wet, the charge may travel through the water and
cause shocks. This is why you should never use electric
devices in the bath or shower. Keep electric appliances dry
and away from water or drinks that might spill.

Electricians are the professionals who work with electricity
and electrical objects. They always wear protective
equipment while at work for their own safety. Special
insulated gloves and rubber-soled boots help to prevent
shocks and electrocutions. As it is made from insulating
materials, the protective clothing immediately stops a current
from travelling through the body.

If you get caught in a lightning storm, remember that
lightning will always travel by the quickest route, even if it
means travelling through an object, such as a building or a
tree. Go indoors or, if you are in a flat area with no shelter,
lie down on the ground. If you are in an outdoor pool, leave
the water straight away.

Saving electricity

We use a lot of electricity to light and heat our homes, as well as to power many electrical devices, like washing machines, phones and computers.

However, it is important not to waste electric energy. Not only does electricity cost money, but it also costs the planet. The less electricity we use, the fewer precious natural resources we use up. And if power plants need to make less electricity, they will burn less fuel and create less air pollution, and we will therefore contribute less to climate change and global warming.

There are lots of little things you can do to help reduce your use of electricity. You can turn off the lights when you leave a room, and turn the computer or television off completely after you have finished using them.

A lot of electricity is used for heating, as well. Heating your home to a slightly lower temperature helps to save energy. Close doors and curtains to conserve heat, and put on a cosy jumper instead of using an electric heater!

If everyone saves a little electricity, it will add up to a lot!

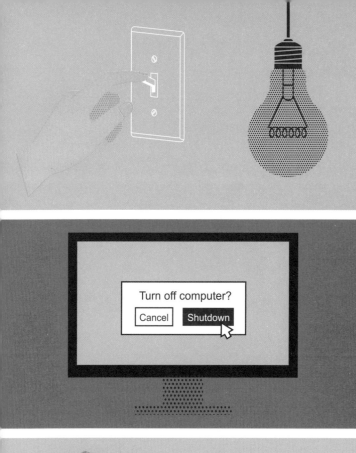

Turn off computer?

Cancel   Shutdown

A Ladybird Book

collectable books for curious kids

Animal Habitats

9780241416860

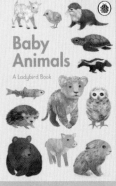

Baby Animals

9780241416907

Insects and Minibeasts

9780241417034

Sea Creatures

9780241417072

SERIES 208

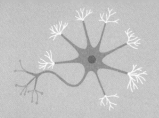

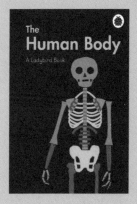

The Human Body

9780241416983

The Solar System

9780241417133

Trains

9780241417171

Weather

9780241417362

SERIES 218